Why
Were You
BORN?

Is there PURPOSE for human life?
Does life, after all, have real
meaning? Here is the awesome
truth!

AUDREY
    ON WEDNESDAY APRIL 24, 1991
WE WERE FULLY AWARE THAT YOU
HAVE TRULY BEEN VERY INSTRUMENTAL
IN CONTRIBUTING TO THE HEALTH
AND HAPPINESS OF YOUR FAMILY,
ADELINE AND AUGIE AND MANY
OTHERS.

Original text by Herbert W. Armstrong (1892-1986)
© 1957, 1972 Worldwide Church of God
All Rights Reserved
Printed in U.S.A.

ISBN 0-943093-77-5

WAS HUMANITY created and put here on the earth by an intelligent and Almighty Creator for a definite purpose? And if so, what is that purpose—and why is humanity so totally unaware of it?

Or, on the other hand, did human life develop, over a period of millions of years, from lower animal species, by a process of evolution? Did we humans come to be formed and shaped as we are purely by natural causes and resident forces?

These are the two possibilities of origins. Today the theory of evolution has gained almost universal acceptance in levels of higher learning.

Yet proponents of the evolutionary doctrine cannot agree on any definite purpose for the presence of the human family on this planet. Neither can they agree on why man is as he is—possessing such awesome intellectual and productive powers—but at the same time being so utterly helpless before the onslaught of this world's problems, sufferings and evils. For that matter, neither has religion adequately shown man his true purpose in life.

It has now become imperative that we find the answer. Humanity's number one problem is now the question of survival. And time is fast running out on us. Why these mounting, fast-accelerating evils?

Neither the evolutionary biologists nor the world's religions have so far given an adequate explanation. They offer no real solutions. They give us no genuine hope!

Question of Survival

We are now in a head-on confrontation with this frightening fact: any one of several heads of nations could plunge this world into the nuclear World War III that could erase all human life from the earth!

Has man progressed to the point where he is about to destroy himself? Is that the end of the evolutionary line? Is that the manner in which science and technology are about to administer the death-blow to all the world's religions?

Is it possible there may exist a source able to shed heretofore unrecognized light on this life-and-death question?

Is it even possible there exists new evidence, vital to humanity's survival and the peace of the world, within the biblical revelation, heretofore unrecognized by Judaism and traditional Christianity? If so, with the imminent possibility of the obliteration of humanity, and time running out, there is no time to be lost in searching it out.

In this crisis hour of human existence, no apology is offered for turning the spotlight on the truly startling revelation that has been rejected by science and higher education, and those vital truths overlooked by religion.

The book called the Holy Bible itself lays claim to being the revelation of basic, necessary knowledge—the instruction manual which man's Maker sent along with the crowning product of his making—mankind!

Could this least-understood of all books reveal purpose behind the presence of mankind on the earth? Does it explain why man is as he is—at once so creative and yet so destructive? Does it explain why man is so utterly helpless before his own problems, yet with such awesome intellectual and productive powers? Does it offer solutions? Does it give us hope?

Emphatic Answers

To all these vital questions, the emphatic answer is a resounding yes! But ask the same questions concerning evolution, or the teachings of religions, and the answer is regrettably no!

Would it not, then, seem the folly of fools to refuse honest examination of these desperately needed answers?

Here, then, is our Maker's crucial message to mankind in this crisis hour of human history.

Expect surprises!

How this missing dimension in knowledge could have been overlooked these millenniums by religion, science and education is as shocking as the fact that our Creator, in the first two chapters of his revealed Instruction Book, tells us clearly and emphatically, that man is neither an animal, nor an immortal soul!

These first two chapters of Genesis clearly dispute the theory of evolution:

The very first verse of the first chapter in the Bible states positively that God exists—and that he created the heaven and the earth. The first chapter also states positively that man is not descended from lower animal species, and that man is not an animal. And the second chapter depicts God himself saying positively that man is not an immortal soul—contrary to the very foundational belief of many, or most, religions!

The very first words in the Bible are: "In the beginning God created the heavens and the earth" (Gen. 1:1, *New King James Version*). No "perhapses"—no theories—just a positive statement!

Another important revelation to note at the very beginning: The human being inspired in the original writing of those words was Moses. Moses wrote in the Hebrew language. The English word "God" is translated from the Hebrew *Elohim*—a noun, plural in form, but with either singular or plural usage. It means in this context one God. But more than one Person compose that one God—just as a family is one family, but may be composed of two, five or more persons.

YOU Are NOT an Animal

Now notice, in verse 21 of Genesis 1: "And God created great whales ... after their kind, and every winged fowl after his kind. . . ." Then in verse 25: "And God made the beast of the earth after his kind, and cattle after their kind. . . ." And then verse 26: "And God said, Let us make man in our image, after our likeness . . ." (*Authorized Version* throughout unless otherwise specified).

This says plainly God made whales after the whale kind, birds after the bird kind, cattle after the cattle kind, chimps after the chimp kind—but God made man after the GOD kind!

And notice, *Elohim* did not say, "Let *me* make man after *my* kind," but, "Let *us* make man in *our* image, after *our* likeness." It is the spokesman of the God kingdom who is speaking. (But let me explain here, that beginning with verse 4 in the second chapter of Genesis, a new and different name for God is introduced. In the Hebrew it is YHWH *Elohim*. In the *Authorized* or *King James Version*, the Hebrew YHWH is translated "Lord"—always in capital letters. So in Genesis 2:4 it is there translated "Lord God."

The Moffatt translation renders it "the Eternal." Actually, this is the name, used in the Hebrew, for the same Person in the God family who appears as *Logos* in the Greek of the New Testament (John 1:1-3), and is translated "the Word." YHWH or Yahweh, is the One of the God family who is the Spokesman, by whom God (the Father of the God family) created all things. It is the One who came in human flesh, Jesus Christ.

This reveals clearly, beyond dispute, that man is not an animal! Man was made in the image and likeness of God—in the very form and shape of God. Man was made to have a relation to God—a link to God—totally unlike any animal. That will become more apparent as we proceed.

But why did God make man in his own image? Why did he create the human species at all?

Was there special purpose? Is there a meaning to human life, unrealized by mankind?

Man, it seems, fails to understand that purpose.

Now look about you. Look at all the species and forms of living creatures. How many of those are able to think, plan, devise, and then bring about, by making or creating, that which was thought out, designed and planned?

Instinct, Instead of Mind

By instinct, beavers build dams. But all these dams follow the same pattern. The beaver cannot think out some new, different pattern and make some new and different thing. Ants may form ant hills; gophers, snakes and rodents dig holes; birds build nests. But they always follow the same pattern. There is no originality, no designing of a new idea, no new construction.

The beavers' dams, the ants' hills, the gophers', snakes' and rodents' holes, the birds' nests are all made by instinct, not by original design.

Take for example an experiment made with weaver birds. For five successive generations, weaver birds were kept in a place with no nest-building material available to them. The fifth generation had never seen a nest. But when nest-building materials, along with other materials, were made accessible, that fifth generation immediately made nests.

And they were weaver-bird nests—not robins' nests or swallows' nests or eagles' nests.

Evolution cannot adequately account for the fact that even the higher animals, equipped as they are with marvelous instinct, lack the unique mind power of man. Nor can it account adequately for the absence of such remarkable instincts in man. Or, for the vast gulf between the powers of animal brain and human mind.

Man can design and build great dams such as the Grand Coulee in Washington State, in the Pacific Northwest. Man can build great tunnels under mountains or rivers. Man can invent and build automobiles, airplanes, battleships, submarines. Man alone, of all God created, is capable of approaching real creative powers.

How Man has Used His Powers

Look, however, at what man has actually done with the things he has had the intelligence and ability to produce.

Thousands of years ago he learned to deal in iron, steel, and other metals. He made implements, constructed buildings—but he also made swords and spears and went out to destroy!

Man learned how to organize his kind into cities, groups, nations. But to what use did he put the organization he controlled?

He organized the able-bodied of his men into armies, and set out to conquer, to destroy, and to acquire by taking rather than by producing and creating.

Man discovered that the powers he possesses allow him to produce explosives, so that he could move mountains if necessary—but soon he began to exert the most frenzied energies of his nations, at incredible expense, endeavoring to develop nuclear weapons faster than his enemies—and now he has already produced weapons of mass destruction that can blast all human life off the earth!

A philosophic country doctor once said to me it was his belief that everything man's hand had ever touched of God's creation man had polluted, befouled, besmirched, and ruined. That statement seemed radical then. But I have been observing, since he said that, and I am almost persuaded he was right. Just look about you, and observe. If you are a thinker, you'll see how man, endowed with a portion of God's actual creative power—and the only being on this planet that has it—turns this power of devising, planning, inventing, and producing into destructive channels.

Look at the great factories of the major industrial nations. Here hums and bustles the creative activity of mankind. Man has made some slight approach toward actual God powers, and God activity, in his tremendous industrial development.

But there is one deadly fault with all this.

Man has learned to exercise scientific, inventive and mechanical powers in excess of his development in ability to direct the product of his efforts into right and constructive channels!

Did GOD Make Man So Destructive?

Why did an all-wise Creator put man on this earth? Did the Creator design and make man as he is—with such tremendous intellect and creative powers, yet so destructive, and so helpless before his most important problems?

It may come as a shock to learn the true explanations of

revolting world conditions, their causes—how it all came about—and of the real purpose for human existence. But read in your own Bible with your own eyes scriptures heretofore overlooked or rejected by man—yet true revelations that have been there all along! More, the Bible itself tells us—if we will listen—how it came about that these foundational, basic truths have been both rejected and overlooked.

Amazing?

Amazing indeed!

But now see it for yourself! If you do not have a Bible, borrow or buy one without delay!

One of the very first things we need to realize, that has been utterly overlooked in the Bible, is this:

The creation of Adam was not completed!

The first chapter of Genesis—called the "creation" chapter—actually does not record the completed creation at all! Man's creation was not finished! Read that amazing statement again! Be sure you understand!

What was created, as revealed in Genesis 1, was the physical creation—the mortal, physical man and woman—the physical material with which to create the spiritual creation!

The Bible plainly reveals this, as we shall see: What God actually is creating in the human family is the crowning, supreme masterpiece of all his works of creation! And that will be—when finished—thousands of millions of humans converted into perfect spiritual character!

The spiritual creation is still in progress!

As covered above, God created Adam and Eve in God's own image, after God's likeness. He created animal life, each after its own animal kind. But he created man after the God kind. That is, as to form and shape, and in intellect, but not of spirit composition.

Man Is Physical

In Genesis 2:7, it is plainly stated: "And the Lord God formed man of the dust of the ground, and breathed into his nostrils the breath of life; and man [physical matter] became a living soul."

When God caused breath—air—to be breathed through

man's nostrils, that man—composed of physical matter from the ground—became a soul. The soul is composed of matter—not of spirit.

That's not what most people believe. But it is what the Bible says! Further it says: "The soul that sinneth, it shall die" (Ezek. 18:4). That is so important it is stated twice, for emphasis: "The soul that sinneth, it shall die" (Ezek. 18:20).

... But God Is Spirit

God is composed of spirit—not of physical matter (John 4:24). But nowhere does the Bible say man is a spirit. Nowhere in the Bible can you find the expression "immortal soul," or "immortality of the soul." In Genesis 1, animals are called souls—that is, Moses used the Hebrew word *nephesh,* which in Genesis 2:7 is translated into the English word "soul," while in Genesis 1:20, 21, 24 it is three times translated "creature."

Now continue with Genesis 2:8, "And the Lord God planted a garden eastward in Eden: and there he put the man whom he had formed. And out of the ground made the Lord God to grow every tree that is pleasant to the sight, and good for food; the tree of life also in the midst of the garden, and the tree of knowledge of good and evil" (verse 9).

"And the Lord God commanded the man, saying, Of every tree of the garden thou mayest freely eat: but of the tree of the knowledge of good and evil, thou shalt not eat of it: for in the day that thou eatest thereof thou shalt surely die" (verses 16-17).

Notice, for disobedience, God said, "Thou shalt surely die"! Man is mortal, and shall die! God said so!

Now what have we seen? God made man mortal—composed of physical matter. In Genesis 3:19 God said to Adam: "... for dust thou art, and unto dust shalt thou return." He was speaking to the conscious man—to the human mind.

Notice what is symbolized and revealed here. The tree of life symbolized eternal life (Gen. 3:22). They did not, as yet, possess immortal life. This was freely offered to Adam and Eve as God's gift.

But they were required to make a choice.

Also in the garden was another tree with symbolic meaning—the tree of "the knowledge of good and evil." To make the wrong choice of taking of that forbidden tree would impose the penalty of death. "Thou shalt surely die," said God—if they chose to disobey and take of that tree.

In other words, as we read in Romans 6:23: "For the wages of sin is death; but the gift of God is eternal life...." This clearly shows that God revealed the gospel—the good news of eternal life in the kingdom of God—to our first parents. And what is the Bible definition of sin? "Sin is," it is written in I John 3:4, "the transgression of the law."

Actually, there exist, overall, only two basic ways of life—two divergent philosophies. They travel in opposite directions. I state them very simply: One is the way of give—the other of get.

More specifically, the one is the way of humility, and of outgoing concern for others equal to self-concern. It is the way of cooperation, serving, helping, sharing; of consideration, patience and kindness. More important, it is also the way of obedience to, reliance on, and worship solely toward God. It is the God-centered way, of love toward God and love toward neighbor.

The opposite is the self-centered way of vanity, lust and greed; of competition and strife; of envy, jealousy, and unconcern for the welfare of others.

Few realize this vital fact: The "give" way is actually an invisible, yet inexorable, spiritual law in active motion. It is summarized by the Ten Commandments.

The CAUSE of Peace and Happiness

It is a law as real, as inflexibly relentless as gravity! It governs and regulates all human relationships!

Why should it seem incongruous that man's Maker—the Creator of all matter, force and energy—the Creator of the laws of physics and chemistry, gravity and inertia—should also have created and set in motion this spiritual law to cause every good result for man?

If the Creator is a God of love—if our Maker is a God of all power—could he possibly have done otherwise? Could he have neglected to provide a way—a cause—to produce peace, happiness, prosperity, successful lives?

There has to be a cause for every effect.

If there is to be peace, happiness, abundant well-being, something must cause it! God could not be God without providing a cause for every desired good.

Isn't it about time we realized that in love for the mankind he created, God also created and set inexorably in motion this spiritual law to provide the cause of every good result?

Let's recapitulate: death is the penalty of sin. Sin is the transgression of God's law! To transgress this law is to reject the way that would cause the good all humans want—to turn to the way that causes every evil result. God forbade Adam and Eve to take the fruit of the tree of the knowledge of good and evil, under penalty of death.

Why? Because he wanted them to choose the way of every desired good—because he wanted them to avoid causing evils, sorrows, pains, suffering, unhappiness. Therefore, taking this fruit was symbolic of transgressing God's spiritual law!

To have taken of the tree of life would have been merely symbolic of receiving the gift of God's Holy Spirit, the very love of God (Rom. 5:5) which fulfills this spiritual law (Rom. 13:10) and which God gives only to those who strive to obey his law (Acts 5:32).

Consider further: A just God could not have warned the first humans of the death penalty without having fully revealed to them the spiritual law—the law later codified as the Ten Commandments—the transgression of which carried that penalty. Bear in mind that the details are not written here—only the highly condensed overall summary of what God taught them.

So God had explained fully to Adam and Eve his way of life—the "give way"—his inexorable spiritual law. God had already set in motion the law that causes all good. He had explained also the way that causes evils—the transgression of that law—else he could not have told them that for transgression they would surely pay the penalty—death.

More clearly stated, God gave man his own choice. He could choose to cause every good and to receive eternal life in happiness. Or, he could choose to cause evils. It is humanity—not God—that causes all the evils that befall man. The choice is man's. What man sows, that does he reap.

Yet here's the crucial point: It was necessary for them to take his word for it—the spiritual law is as invisible as gravity and inertia! They could not see this law. But God had told them the way of good, and the way of evil.

Now come to chapter 3 in Genesis.

"Now the serpent was more subtil than any beast of the field which the Lord God had made . . ." (verse 1).

Much of the Bible is in symbols—but the Bible explains its own symbols. It is, of course, very out-of-date to believe in a devil today, but the Bible plainly speaks of a devil, named Satan. In Revelation 12:9 and 20:2, the symbol of a serpent is plainly explained to represent the devil. (Write for our free booklet *Did God Create a Devil?*)

Notice, now, the temptation.

The Subtle Temptation

Satan subtly went first to the woman. He got to the man through his wife.

"And he said unto the woman, Yea, hath God said, Ye shall not eat of every tree of the garden? And the woman said unto the serpent, We may eat of the fruit of the trees of the garden: but of the fruit of the tree which is in the midst of the garden, God hath said, Ye shall not eat of it, neither shall ye touch it, lest ye die. And the serpent said unto the woman, Ye shall not surely die: for God doth know that in the day ye eat thereof, then your eyes shall be opened, and ye shall be as gods [Hebrew: *Elohim,* God], knowing good and evil" (verses 1-5).

The narration here attributes astute subtlety to the devil. First, he discredited God. In effect, he said, "You can't rely on God's word. He said you are mortal and can die. He knows better than that; he knows your minds are so perfect that you can be God."

It is the prerogative of God alone to determine what is right and what is sin—what is good and what is evil. God has not delegated to man the right or power to decide what is sin—but he compels us to decide whether to sin, or to obey his Law.

So that all could rightly determine what is good the creative power had to produce and set in motion inexorable spiritual law—a law which automatically causes good if obeyed, and evils when disobeyed!

Adam and Eve had only God's word that they were mortal and could die. Now Satan disputed this. He said they were immortal souls.

Whom should they believe? They had no proof, except God's word. But now Satan discredited that, and claimed just the opposite.

Satan said their intellectual powers were so great they could determine for themselves what is good and what is evil. That is a God-prerogative. "You can be God!" said Satan.

Thus Satan was appealing to their human vanity. Remember, they had just been created, with perfect human minds. Not God minds—but perfect human minds. They allowed the thought to enter their minds that they possessed intellectual powers so great that they could assume the God-prerogative of producing the knowledge of what is good and what is evil!

Intellectual vanity seized them. They were enthralled, intoxicated with vanity at the grand prospect.

How, after all, could they be sure God had told them the truth?

They saw (verse 6)—they used observation—that the forbidden tree was good for food, pleasant to their eyes, and desired to make them wise. Intellectual vanity was stirred. In their vanity they put their trust in human reason. They decided to reject revelation imparted by God, and to make the very first scientific experiment!

They took the forbidden fruit and ate it.

They took to themselves the prerogative of deciding what is good, and what is evil. In so doing, they rejected the God-centered way of God's spiritual law, and, rejecting it, of necessity they chose the way that transgresses it.

They pioneered in deciding for themselves what is right and what is wrong—what is righteousness and what is sin. And humanity has been doing what seems right in its own eyes ever since.

And how did they do it? They 1) rejected revelation and

relied totally on 2) observation, 3) experimentation and 4) human reason. And that is precisely the basic method of reasoning used by modern man!

And the final result of that experiment? They died! But not before producing the first child delinquent—the first criminal and murderer: Cain, who slew his brother Abel (Gen. 4:8).

The most vital dimension of knowledge was missing from their "scientific" procedure!

Much Beyond Human Power to Discover

There is much vital, basic and important knowledge beyond the powers of man to discover! Such important knowledge as what man is, why man is—why he was put on earth and for what purpose. And if there is purpose, what is that purpose? And how may we attain it? What is the way to peace? Most nations seek and strive for peace—yet none finds it—they have war! What are the true values in life? This world pursues the false values!

Those are the most basic and important things man needs to know. Yet he may search for the answers in vain. He can know them only through revelation.

Then such knowledge as: how the earth came to be, when it came to be, how old is human life upon it—the mystery of origins. These questions absorb the time, thought, research and thinking of scientists, philosophers, historians—yet these learned individuals can come up only with guesses, hypotheses, theories, but no proof—the definite knowledge they could know only by revelation.

In taking to themselves the forbidden fruit, the first humans took to themselves the determination of what is good and what is evil. In so doing, they rejected the fact that God's living, inexorable spiritual law is the way of good—the cause of all good—and its transgression the way of evil—the cause of all evil. Since they and humanity in general after them have taken to themselves the determination of what is good, they of necessity have followed the way contrary to God's Law. They have followed the way that has produced all the vast mountain of evils that has formed in this sick, sick world!

They made themselves competitors of the living God. That is why it is written in Romans 8:7: "The carnal mind [the natural mind we all have] is enmity [hostile] against God: for it is not subject to the law of God, neither indeed can be."

What IS the Missing Dimension?

So what, then, is the missing dimension in all knowledge?

It is revelation from God!

For even though rejected by the first humans—even though rejected by mankind in general—God did bequeath to mankind his revelation of basic knowledge. We have it in writing! The Holy Bible is that revelation. It contains history, instruction, inspiration and prophecy.

It does not contain all knowledge. It contains that basic, foundational knowledge otherwise inaccessible to man.

What, then, is wrong with knowledge production today? The most vital dimension is missing! Error generally comes from assuming a false premise, taken carelessly for granted without proof, and then building on that premise. And when the basic hypothesis or premise is false, the entire structure built upon it is defective!

The tools of modern science are observation, experimentation, and reason. Are those tools wrong? Not at all! The error comes from rejection of revelation. For revelation is the true starting premise. When man substitutes his own false hypotheses, the most vital dimension in the knowledge production is missing.

God's Word—his instruction manual for mankind—is the foundation of all knowledge. It is not the sum-total of knowledge. It is the foundation—the true premise—the starting point—the concept that directs the approach to the acquisition of further knowledge.

Man Should Produce Knowledge

God intended man to produce additional knowledge. He gave us the basis—the foundation—the premise—the concept. But he also provided us with eyes with which to observe. With hands and feet to explore and measure. With means to produce laboratories, test-tubes, experimentation. He gave us awesome minds with which to think.

If a plane from London destined for New York starts off in the wrong direction, it will not reach the right destination. It is just as important to start off in the right direction, from the true premise, with the right approach, in this matter of knowledge production.

God intended man to use observation, experimentation, and human reason. He supplied us with the basis—the foundation—the start in the right direction, with the right concept. But our first parents rejected the most vital dimension in all knowledge. And mankind has continued to reject the very foundation of all knowledge. Knowledge production has been operating without a foundation—based on false premises and erroneous hypotheses.

That is why human knowledge production has failed to solve humanity's problems, and to cure the world's ills.

Manufacturers of mechanical or electrical appliances send along an instruction manual with their product. The Bible is our Maker's instruction manual which he has sent along with the product of his making—humanity.

Six thousand years of human misery, unhappiness and evils ought to provide sufficient proof for those willing to see, that humanity, starting with our first parents, rejected the most vital dimension.

Compelled to Choose

Now remember, I said creation is still going on. Adam was freely offered eternal life. He was compelled to make a choice. Had he and Eve made the choice to believe God— accept knowledge from God, instead of taking to themselves the determination of the knowledge of what is good and what is evil—they could have taken of the tree of life.

That tree symbolically represented the Holy Spirit of God. Taking it would have impregnated within them God-life—spirit-life. Then Adam's creation would have been completed within his life-time. He would ultimately have been changed from mortal to immortal—from physical material composition to being composed of spirit, even as God is!

But the first humans rejected basic revelation of knowledge from God—just as humanity has done ever since. They rejected the way God set in motion to cause peace, prosperity, happiness and joy. They limited the acquisition of knowledge to their human minds.

And ever since, man has tried to go his own way—governing himself—living the "get" way, with unconcern for the good of others. And man's way has resulted in all the mountain of evils that has been built up in this world.

Therein is the explanation of all the illiteracy, the poverty, the disease and squalor of the world's majority.

Therein is the explanation of the evils that exist in the "more advanced" and "developed" areas of the world. They have education—but with a great, vast dimension missing! Education with no knowledge of the purpose of life. Education that can produce computers, fly missions into space and back, but cannot solve man's problems.

And why? Because the problems are spiritual and man has rejected the knowledge of God's spiritual law—the way of life that would cause peace and universal good!

But has God left stricken humanity to its fate?

By no means.

God's spiritual creation is still in progress.

The real answer was brought out by Job. "If a man die, shall he live again?" Job asked—and answered: "All the days of my appointed time will I wait, till my change come. Thou shalt call, and I will answer thee: thou wilt have a desire to the work of thine hands" (Job 14:14-15).

The latter part of his quotation, most often overlooked, is the key to this whole riddle. Read it again!

"Thou wilt have a desire to the work of thine hands"!

Study that! Job knew he was merely the work of God's hands. Merely a piece of divine workmanship in the hands of the Creator. Merely a piece of plastic clay in the hands of the Master Potter.

We Are God's Workmanship

The prophet Isaiah explains this also: "But now, O Lord, thou art our father; we are the clay, and thou our potter; and we all are the work of thy hand" (Isa. 64:8).

And in calling us forth from the grave, in the resurrection, God will have a desire to finish the work of his hands. The model, from which the finished spiritual product is to be molded, is material substance—mortal human clay.

In the creation of Genesis 1, God formed and shaped man physically, into God's image. But we do not, as humans, have the spiritual character of the perfect God. During this life-time, for those whom God calls, if they yield and respond, God begins to re-form and shape them spiritually, while they become more and more like him in spiritual character.

For this grand and glorious purpose, God has marked out a duration of seven thousand years! Each 24-hour day of the Genesis 1 creation was a type of one of the seven millennial days of the spiritual creation.

Except for those whom God specially and individually calls, for the first six millennial days, God leaves man to write his lesson in human experience. Man made the choice of relying on himself under sway and influence of Satan. God is allowing man to demonstrate beyond question his helpless-ness—without God's Holy Spirit—to live in a way that pro-duces peace, happiness, and universal abundance.

Or, the parallel: God is allowing Satan the six millennial days for his labor of deception and evil. And on the seventh millennial day he shall not be allowed to do any of his evil work—he shall be imprisoned (Rev. 20:1-3), while the living Christ brings truth and salvation to the world.

Now let's look briefly at the importance of redemption in all this. What is redemption?

We read in Ephesians 2:8, 10 "By grace are ye saved through faith. . . . For we are his workmanship, created in Christ Jesus unto good works, which God hath before or-dained that we should walk in them". Notice, there are good works to salvation.

The "we" in New Testament language usually means Christians—those truly converted. We, then, are God's work-manship. Yes! "Created"—now being created—to what objec-tive—to what purpose? Note it! "Unto good works"! Unto perfect spiritual character!

Now the apostle Paul here is not speaking of Adam's creation, six thousand years ago. He is speaking of Chris-tians, now, being created—unto good works. We are his workmanship—the Creator is still creating. He is molding, fashioning, changing us, transforming us to his own noble, righteous, holy, spiritual character. Yes, creating in us this perfect character.

Redemption, therefore, is a process!

But how "the god of this world" (II Cor. 4:4) would blind your eyes to that! He tries to deceive you into thinking all there is to it is just "accepting Christ"—with "no works"—and presto-chango, you're pronounced "saved."

The Bible reveals that "he that shall endure unto the end, the same shall be saved" (Matt. 24:13).

"Therefore if any man be in Christ, he is a new creature . . ." (II Cor. 5:17). Yes, a new creation!

"And be renewed in the spirit of your mind; and that ye put on the new man, which after God is [being] created in righteousness and true holiness" (Eph. 4:23-24).

It all begins in the faculty we call the mind. Repentance, the first step in salvation, is a change of mind. We believe through the mind. The receiving and indwelling of the Holy Spirit is a renewing of the mind. Gradually, through Bible study, learning to live by "every Word of God," being continually corrected, keeping in constant prayer, the yielded person acquires the very mind of God. And thus the new man—a holy, spiritual character—is being created in righteousness, and in true holiness.

Born Again . . . HOW?

In this new creation God works in man, the man must be "born again."

God made Adam out of matter. Jesus said to Nicodemus, "That which is born of the flesh is flesh"! Then he explained we must be born again to enter into the kingdom of God. Not again of the flesh—not entering our mother's womb, as Nicodemus thought he meant—but born of the Spirit—born of God. As we were born of the flesh from a fleshly human father, so now we must be born of the Spirit by God, the heavenly spiritual Father.

And this process is brought about, in God's great purpose, by a person first coming to see how wrong are the ways of mortal humans, thinking and living contrary to the revealed laws of God. The first stage is repentance. Surrender to Almighty God!

But we now are the "clay models," in the hands of the Master Potter.

If in this life our thinking, our ways, are changed until we really do become—in spiritual character—new creatures in Christ Jesus, conformed to his will, then that clay model, worked over, fashioned and shaped as God would have it, is finally turned into the finished spiritual creation.

This entire creation, therefore, begins in Christ and is finished by him.

God created all things by Jesus Christ (Eph. 3:9). Jesus was the workman, then, who created the original Adam. But our spiritual creation begins in him, too. He it is who became our living Example—who came into the world to lead the way—and became the firstborn from among the dead (Rom. 8:29)—the first completed, perfected spiritual man.

Now come to the ultimate purpose of human life on the earth.

It is stupendous beyond the capacity, perhaps, for many to grasp. But see it, with your own eyes, in your own Bible!

Each year, on the Sunday called "Easter," millions celebrate the resurrection of Christ. But do they really believe that he was asleep in death and therefore rose from the dead? The Bible says he rose from the dead!

But how many believe he has been alive ever since? How many believe the very Christ who died is alive today? How many know what he has been doing these past 1,900 years?

DO YOU?

The entire book of Hebrews is devoted to telling us what he has been doing, what he is doing now, and what he will do in the future.

Read it in your Bible. Expect shocking surprises—happy surprises!

Begin at the beginning—chapter 1, verse 1: "God, who at sundry times and in divers manners spake in time past unto the fathers by the prophets, hath in these last days spoken unto us by his Son, whom he hath appointed heir of all things, by whom also he made the worlds...."

The "all things" refers to the entire universe, as translated in the Moffatt translation.

Continuing the same sentence, ". . . who being the brightness of his glory, and the express image of his person. . . ." Moffatt translates that "express image" as "stamped with God's own character." Continue: ". . . and upholding all things by the word of his power. . . ." (verses 2-3).

Moffatt translates that as sustaining the whole universe by the word of his power.

In other words, God Almighty, the Father of the kingdom of God—which is the divine family of God—has appointed the resurrected, living Christ, his Son, as Chief Executive in the administration of the government of God over the entire vast universe!

Several times, in the Bible, converted Christians, in whom is God's Holy Spirit, are called heirs of God, and joint-heirs with Jesus Christ (Rom. 8:17; Gal. 3:29; 4:7; Titus 3:7, etc.). Now could that mean we are appointed to share that rulership of the entire vast universe with Christ?

Begin now with Hebrews 2:6, quoting from Psalms 8:4-6: the question is asked: "What is man, that thou art mindful of him?"

Yes, what is there about sinning, mortal man that God should be concerned about him?

What are you—that God should be concerned about you? Note well the incredible answer.

The Transcendent Purpose

"Thou madest him a little lower than the angels." Yes, now, much higher than animals, but still lower than angels who are composed of spirit (see chapter 1:5-7, 13-14).

Continue, Hebrews 2:7: ". . . thou crownedst him with glory and honour, and didst set him over the works of thy hands: thou hast put all things in subjection under his feet. For in that he put all in subjection under him, he left nothing that is not put under him . . ." (verse 8).

In chapter 1, quoted above, "all things" is also translated "the universe." Could it mean God has put the entire vast universe under man? That has been too utterly fantastic for even theologians to believe! But notice the last sentence in that verse: "But now we see not yet all things put under him."

That explains it. God has not yet put the vastness of the universe under man's control and governing. Not while we are still human! Man has so far proved he is incapable of even governing himself, here on the earth! No, we don't see man yet in such fantastic power.

But what do we see, now?

Next verse, the 9th: "But we see Jesus, who was made a little lower than the angels . . ."—mortal, like we are now—". . . for the suffering of death, crowned with glory and honour . . ."—as explained in the first chapter—crowned—the executive ruler over the universe—". . . that he by the grace of God should taste death for every man. For it became him, for whom are all things, and by whom are all things, in bringing many sons unto glory, to make the captain of their salvation perfect through sufferings" (Heb. 2:10).

Do you grasp what that says?

"In bringing many sons unto glory." We humans who repent, come to believe God—believe what he says—believe what he reveals—believe the knowledge he reveals to us, now, through the Bible—instead of rejecting knowledge from him as Adam and Eve did—as most in science and higher education do—we become God's sons when he puts within us his Holy Spirit. We are the sons he is bringing to this supreme glory!

How Christ Was Made Perfect

Now grasp this: ". . . to make the captain of their salvation. . . ." Christ is the captain of our salvation. Or, that may be translated also as the pioneer, who has gone on ahead, before us, into this matchless glory. He already has inherited all things—the universe!

But notice further: "to make the captain of their salvation perfect"—how? How was even Christ made perfect?—"through sufferings"!

And notice, in verse 11: ". . . he is not ashamed to call them brethren." Christ, in glory, is not ashamed to call us—who have his Spirit—who rely on and obey him—brethren!

"Though he were a Son, yet learned he obedience by the

things which he suffered; and being made perfect, he became the author of eternal salvation unto all them that obey him" (Heb. 5:8-9).

There it is again. Jesus is the author of our salvation—he wrote that salvation by his experience—he was the first human ever to achieve it—to be perfected, finished as a perfect character!

Jesus learned! He suffered! But out of it came perfection.

Do you see?

Do you begin to understand?

Satan did not upset God's plan. All that has happened, God permitted—for a purpose. Redemption is not a repairing of the damage—not a restoring to a condition "just as good" as Adam before the "fall." No, that was merely the beginning—the material creation. Redemption is the great spiritual creation. By it, God is creating in us something infinitely superior to Adam before he sinned.

Do you see now what God is creating, in you and me?

He is creating something higher than angels or archangels. He is creating the supreme masterpiece of all God's creation . . . holy, perfect spiritual character.

And what is character?

What Spiritual Righteous Character Is

Perfect character, such as God is creating in us, will result in a person finally made immortal, who is a separate entity from God; who, through independent free choice has come to know, and to choose, and to do, what is right. And that means to believe and know that what God instructs is what is right.

Inanimate rocks will roll downhill by power of gravity. Water runs in its channels through creeks and rivers into oceans. Great planets, some many times larger than the earth, must travel in God's ordained course. These things are marvelous examples of the creative power of God. Yet these things are inanimate—they have no mind, no free choice, no character.

Animals do not sin. They do not know enough to sin. They act by instinct, or according to training of others. They do not have this character.

Character is the possession and practice of love, patience, mercy, faith, kindness, gentleness, meekness, temperance, self-restraint, and right self-direction. Character involves knowledge, wisdom, purpose, ability, all properly controlled and developed, and through independent choice.

Holy, righteous character is something that is developed only through experience. Experience requires time, and circumstances. And so God creates time and God creates circumstances which produce character.

So God first formed out of dust—out of matter—the flesh-and-blood man, in the image of God ("image" in Genesis 1:27 means form, or shape, not composition). And through seven thousand years of experience, God is taking the human family through a process, the results of which, even "as we have borne the image of the earthy [mortal Adam], we shall also bear the image of the heavenly"— Christ Jesus immortal, the "second" Adam—(I Cor. 15:49).

Yes, once fashioned, shaped, molded according to God's purpose, even we shall be like him, for we shall see him as he is (I John 3:1-2).

WHY All This Human Suffering?

There are just two broad principles of life—God's way, or God's law, summed up in the Ten Commandments, and Satan's way of competition, greed, vanity.

All suffering—all unhappiness, fear, misery, and death— has come from the transgression of God's law. Living by that great law of Love, then, is the only way to peace, happiness, and joy. God placed man on this planet to learn that lesson— to learn it through generations of experience.

Yes, we too learn by suffering. God has revealed the true way—his revelation is, though certainly most human beings have never read it, available to man. But man, given the right of free choice, always has turned his back on God, and God's true way. And even though man as a whole still refuses to see or learn the lesson, he has written this lesson indelibly in the history of human experience.

We learn through experience. And through suffering. This, then, is the very stuff of which character is made.

Once this godly character is developed in us, what shall we be like in the resurrection?

Already, now, in this life, the truly converted Christian, having God's Holy Spirit dwelling within, being led by God's Spirit, is a son of God. In prayer he calls God "Father."

Notice: "Beloved, now are we the sons of God, and it doth not yet appear what we shall be..." (I John 3:2).

What we shall be is not now apparent—does not now appear—is not yet seen. Continue, "...but we know that, when he shall appear, we shall be like him; for we shall [then] see him as he is." Our appearance, then, will be like that of Christ now.

And what does Christ look like, now?

His appearance is described in Revelation 1:14-16: "His head and his hairs were white like wool, as white as snow; and his eyes were as a flame of fire; and his feet like unto fine brass, as if they burned in a furnace; and his voice as the sound of many waters.... and his countenance was as the sun shineth in his strength."

Sinless Spirit Beings

But once actually born of God—entering into his kingdom—his family—by the resurrection, we shall be composed of Spirit. We shall be like God, and like Christ now is, completely sinless.

As Christ was born of God by his resurrection, so shall we be. "For whom he did foreknow, he also did predestinate to be conformed to the image of his Son, that he might be the firstborn among many brethren" (Rom. 8:29).

At that time we shall be changed from mortal to immortal. "For our conversation [citizenship] is in heaven; from whence also we look for the Saviour, the Lord Jesus Christ: who shall change our vile body, that it may be fashioned like unto his glorious body..." (Phil. 3:20-21).

Do you begin to comprehend why you were born? How glorious is the truth!

Now Understand Why You Were Born!

The purpose of life is that in us God is really recreating his own kind—reproducing himself after his own kind—for

we, upon conversion, join the household of God. Then
through study of God's revelation in his Word, living by his
every Word, constant prayer, daily experience with trials and
testings, we grow spiritually more and more like God, until,
at the time of the resurrection we shall be instantaneously
changed from mortal into immortal, composed of spirit—we
shall then be full members of the God family!

For, remember, the Hebrew word translated "God" is
Elohim, a noun plural in form. There is one God—not many
gods. But that one God is a divine family—a kingdom. There
is but one true Church—one Church, but many members
(I Cor. 12:20).

So it is with God.

As an illustration, there is the mineral kingdom, the
plant kingdom, the animal kingdom, the human kingdom, in
this material world. Spiritually, there is the angel kingdom,
and, high above all, the kingdom of God. A human—flesh and
blood—cannot enter into the kingdom of God (John 3:6;
I Cor. 15:50), but one born of God can.

Do you really grasp it? The purpose of your being alive
is that finally you be born into the kingdom of God, which
is the divine family of God.

When you fully grasp this tremendous, wonderful truth,
your mind will be filled with transcendent joy and glory. It
gives a new meaning to life so wonderful you'll never comprehend the full heights of its splendor.

It means, of course, total renunciation, denial, of those
injurious things and ways which have falsely seemed so bright
and alluring to this world.

But your eyes will be open at last to the great deception—the scales will fall from your blinded vision—you'll see
the meaning of life, its great purpose, as you never dreamed
it could be. Giving up this world's evils, temptations and
pitfalls—its snares and delusions which have glittered and
then ended only in sorrow and suffering—is but emerging
from gross darkness into the splendor of true light, and of
happiness and joy forever!

In the words of I Peter 1:8, you will "rejoice with joy
unspeakable and full of glory"!

ADDITIONAL READING

The Worldwide Church of God produces many informative and interesting publications on a wide range of biblical topics. Four are listed below.

The Plain Truth

The bewildering tempo of today's news is greater than one person can keep pace with and digest. *The Plain Truth* magazine spotlights trends, important developments, problems, and tells its readers what is behind the news and where it is leading.

What Do You Mean . . . Salvation?

What is salvation? Is it a place, destination, condition, or reward? Not one in a hundred knows what salvation is or how to receive it. Do you?

Where Are We Now in Prophecy?

The major events that will headline tomorrow's news are already pre-recorded. Yet biblical prophecy is a complete mystery to millions. Here are certain vital keys that will unlock prophecy to your understanding.

Human Nature — Did God Create It?

Here is a bombshell of a truth almost no one has understood! The world's evils are attributed to human nature. But are babies born with this selfish, evil nature? If not, what is its origin?

Write for your personal copies of the above publications. They are sent free as an educational service in the public interest.

A Unique Cours
Understanding

Have you found it difficult—even impossible—to understand what the Bible says? The Ambassador College Bible Correspondence Course can help you begin to comprehend the Bible as never before. More than 2,000,000 people have enrolled in this unique course!

These informative, eye-opening lessons make plain the answers to the "unanswerable" problems facing millions today. They explain the very purpose of human life. You will study the plain truths of your Bible!

You will learn the truth about the purpose of life, about what Bible prophecy says concerning world events today, about the God-inspired way to true happiness. All these topics and more are presented in step-by-step detail. A different major subject is explored in each monthly lesson.

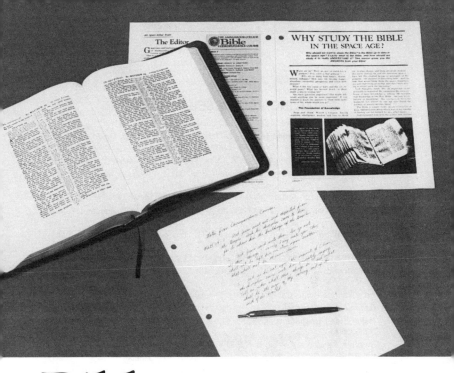

n Bible

And the Bible itself is the only textbook you will need.

You will find each lesson richly rewarding, and periodic quizzes will help you evaluate your progress. There is no tuition fee or obligation—these lessons are absolutely free! Why not request a sample lesson? Send your request in the reply envelope or write to our address nearest you.

Free of Charge

Just mail the reply envelope stitched into this booklet.

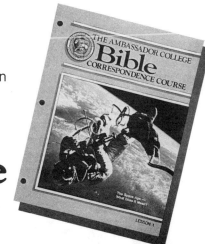

MAILING ADDRESSES WORLDWIDE

United States: Worldwide Church of God, Pasadena, California 91123

United Kingdom, Europe (except as listed) and Middle East: The Plain Truth, P.O. Box 111, Borehamwood, Herts, England WD6 1LU

Canada: Worldwide Church of God, P.O. Box 44, Station A, Vancouver, B.C. V6C 2M2

Canada (French language): Le Monde à Venir, B.P. 121, Succ. A, Montreal, P. Q. H3C 1C5

Mexico: Institución Ambassador, Apartado Postal 5-595, 06502 México D.F.

South America: Institución Ambassador, Apartado Aéreo 11430, Bogotá 1, D.E., Colombia

Caribbean: Worldwide Church of God, G.P.O. Box 6063, San Juan, Puerto Rico 00936-6063

France: Le Monde à Venir, B.P. 64, 75662 Paris Cédex 14, France

Switzerland: Le Monde à Venir, Case Postale 10, 91 rue de la Servette, CH-1211 Genève 7, Suisse

Italy: La Pura Verità, Casella Postale 10349 I-00144 Roma EUR, Italia

Germany: Ambassador College, Postfach 1129, D-5300 Bonn 1, West Germany

Holland and Belgium: Ambassador College, Postbus 444, 3430 AK Nieuwegein, Nederland

Belgium: Le Monde à Venir, B.P. 4031, 6000 Charleroi 4, Belgique

Denmark: The Plain Truth, Box 211, DK-8100 Aarhus C, Denmark

Norway: The Plain Truth, Postboks 2513 Solli, N-0203 Oslo 2, Norway

Sweden: The Plain Truth, Box 5380, S-102 46, Stockholm, Sweden

Finland: The Plain Truth, Box 603, SF-00101 Helsinki, Finland

Australia: Worldwide Church of God, P.O. Box 202, Burleigh Heads, Queensland 4220, Australia

India: Worldwide Church of God, P.O. Box 6727, Bombay 400 052, India

Sri Lanka: Worldwide Church of God, P.O. Box 1824, Colombo, Sri Lanka

Malaysia: The Plain Truth, Locked Bag No. 2002, 41990 Klang, Malaysia

Singapore: Worldwide Church of God, P.O. Box 111, Farrer Road Post Office, Singapore 9128

New Zealand and the Pacific Isles: Ambassador College, P.O. Box 2709, Auckland 1, New Zealand

The Philippines: Worldwide Church of God, P.O. Box 1111, MCPO, 1299 Makati, Metro Manila, Philippines

Israel: Ambassador College, P.O. Box 19111, Jerusalem

South Africa: Ambassador College, P.O. Box 5644, Cape Town 8000, South Africa

Zimbabwe: Ambassador College, Box UA30, Union Avenue, Harare, Zimbabwe

Nigeria: Worldwide Church of God, PMB 21006, Ikeja, Lagos State, Nigeria

Ghana: Worldwide Church of God, P.O. Box 9617, Kotoka International Airport, Accra, Ghana

Kenya: Worldwide Church of God, P.O. Box 47135, Nairobi, Kenya

Mauritius: The Plain Truth, P.O. Box 888, Port Louis, Mauritius

379344/9002/1.2

DELTA